# Gently Dow1

**Martin Sherman** was born in Philadelphia, educated at Boston University and now lives in London. His early plays include *Passing By*, *Cracks*, and *Rio Grande*, all originally presented by Playwrights Horizons in New York. *Bent* premiered at the Royal Court Theatre in 1979, transferred to the Criterion Theatre and was then presented on Broadway, where it received a Tony nomination for Best Play and won the Dramatists Guild's Hull-Warriner Award. *Bent* has been produced in over forty-five countries and has been turned into a ballet in Brazil. In 1989, it was revived at the National Theatre and has been voted one of the NT2000 One Hundred Plays of the Century. His next plays were *Messiah* (Hampstead and Aldwych Theatres, 1983), *When She Danced* (King's Head, 1988; Gielgud, 1991), *A Madhouse in Goa* (Lyric Hammersmith and Apollo, 1989), *Some Sunny Day* (Hampstead, 1996), and *Rose* (National Theatre, 1999). *Rose* received an Olivier nomination for Best Play and transferred to Broadway the following season. Sherman has written an adaptation of E. M. Forster's *A Passage to India* for Shared Experience (Riverside Studios, 2002; Lyric Hammersmith, 2004) and a new version of a Luigi Pirandello play, *Absolutely! (Perhaps)* (Wyndhams, 2003). He has also written the book for the musical *The Boy From Oz*, which opened on Broadway in 2003. His screenplays include *The Clothes in the Wardrobe* (U.S. title: *The Summer House*), *Alive and Kicking*, *Bent*, *Callas Forever*, and *The Roman Spring of Mrs. Stone*. His *Plays: One* was published by Bloomsbury Methuen Drama in 2004 and *Plays: Two* in 2013.

**Martin Sherman**

# Gently Down the Stream

Bloomsbury Methuen Drama
An imprint of Bloomsbury Publishing Plc

B L O O M S B U R Y
LONDON • OXFORD • NEW YORK • NEW DELHI • SYDNEY

**Bloomsbury Methuen Drama**
An imprint of Bloomsbury Publishing Plc
Imprint previously known as Methuen Drama

50 Bedford Square
London
WC1B 3DP
UK

1385 Broadway
New York
NY 10018
USA

www.bloomsbury.com

BLOOMSBURY, METHUEN DRAMA and the Diana logo
are registered trademarks of Bloomsbury Publishing Plc

First published 2017

**British Library Cataloguing-in-Publication Data**
A catalogue record for this book is available from the British Library.

ISBN: PB: 978-1-3500-4062-5
ePDF: 978-1-3500-4063-2
ePub: 978-1-3500-4064-9

**Library of Congress Cataloging-in-Publication Data**
A catalog record for this book is available from the Library of Congress.

Cover design by Olivia d'Cruz    Cover image © Stock/CSA-Printstoc

Typeset by Country Setting, Kingsdown, Kent CT14 8ES
Printed and bound in Great Britain

To find out more about our authors and books visit www.bloomsbury.com.
Here you will find extracts, author interviews, details of forthcoming events
and the option to sign up for our newsletters.

# Gently Down the Stream

*For*
*Tom Erhardt*
*and*
*Judy Chiariello*

*Gently Down the Stream* received its world premiere at The
Public Theater, New York (Oskar Eustis, Artistic Director;
Patrick Willingham, Executive Producer), on March 14, 2017
with the following cast and creative team:

**Beau**          Harvey Fierstein
**Rufus**         Gabriel Ebert
**Harry**         Christopher Sears

*Director*   Sean Mathias
*Assistant director*   David Nathan Perlow
*Scenic designer*   Derek McLane
*Costume designer*   Michael Krass
*Lighting designer*   Peter Kaczorowski
*Sound designers*   Rob Milburn and Michael Bodeen
*Production stage manager*   Scott Rollison
*Assistant stage manager*   Samantha Fremer

*London. 2001. The front room of* **Beau***'s flat in Shepherd's Bush.
There is a piano, and many, many filled bookcases. One door leads
outside; another to a bedroom. There is a kitchenette on the side.* **Beau**
*comes out of the kitchen, carrying two cups of tea. He is sixty-one.*
**Rufus** *comes out of the bathroom, arranging his clothes. He is twenty-
eight.* **Beau** *hands him a cup of tea.*

**Beau**   It's licorice and ginger. With honey and lemon.
I didn't put in the honey and lemon myself, it's part of the
recipe. All in one little teabag. No caffeine, of course.

**Rufus** *sips it.*

**Rufus**   Wicked.

*Pause.*

So . . .

*Pause.*

Tell me about Mabel Mercer.

**Beau**   Sorry?

**Rufus**   Mabel Mercer.

**Beau**   How do you know about . . .

**Rufus** (*grins*)   I know a lot of things.

**Beau**   Most probably. But *Mabel Mercer*?

**Rufus** (*proudly*)   Absolutely. Greatest cabaret singer who
ever lived.

**Beau**   Well, yes, I suppose, but how did you know that I . . .

**Rufus** (*taps his head*)   Ah!

**Beau**   The internet's supposed to be anonymous!

**Rufus**   It is. Except for someone like me. My head is full
of stuff, you know what I mean? Have you done Google yet?
It's a new thing, a search engine. Isn't that a wonderful
phrase? My mind's a search engine. It stores totally useless

facts. Google should install an electric sensor to my brain. I'm going to waste.

**Beau**   I haven't the slightest inkling what you are talking about . . .

**Rufus**   I love your accent . . .

**Beau**   But how did you place me with . . .

**Rufus**   Your photograph. The one on your profile. I recognized you. What did you call yourself?

**Beau**   Don't. I'm embarrassed.

**Rufus**   "Autumn leaf."

**Beau**   You have just subjected me to extreme mortification.

**Rufus**   What part of the South?

**Beau**   What?

**Rufus**   Your accent.

**Beau**   You should know; it's a useless fact.

**Rufus**   But I don't.

**Beau**   New Orleans.

**Rufus**   I thought New Orleans sounded like Southern mixed with Brooklyn.

**Beau**   It does. Keep listening. How did you place me with—

**Rufus**   Mabel?

**Beau**   Yes.

**Rufus**   Someone told me.

**Beau**   Someone told you? This assignation was public knowledge?!

**Rufus**   I love the way you speak.

**Beau**   I repeat . . .

**Rufus** (*smiles*)   "Assignation."

**Beau**   I repeat . . .

**Rufus**   Oh, keep your wig on. (*Gleeful.*) It's not, is it?

*Pulls* **Beau**'s *hair.*

**Beau**   Ouch! (*Sighs.*) You're exasperating.

**Rufus**   It's great you don't dye it. Men look ghoulish with dyed hair, don't you think? People should be proud of their age.

**Beau**   Age. (*Suddenly alert.*) Age! What am I doing with a child?

**Rufus**   I'm hardly a child. I'm twenty-eight. I have a law degree. I'm a serious person.

**Beau**   Nonetheless, I'm old enough to be your ancestor. I shouldn't have gone onto that idiot machine. What kind of name is Gaydar? But then I thought no one would bother with me. And then you popped up, chasing me through cyberspace. Coming on to me. Making very enticing sexual suggestions, I might say. Which I hadn't expected. Not at my age. And, admittedly, it was very flattering, but look at you . . . You're so young you make me feel like a priest.

**Rufus**   But I fancy you.

**Beau**   How can you fancy me?

**Rufus**   I like older . . .

**Beau**   *Old* . . .

**Rufus**   Old men.

**Beau**   This probably has something to do with a father.

**Rufus**   Why are you looking for an explanation?

**Beau**   Or some kind of abuse early on . . .

**Rufus**   No. Nothing like that. I just like older men.

**Beau**   There has to be something lurking in your past . . .

**Rufus**   You're so American.

**Beau**   What does that mean?

**Rufus**   Everything has to have a reason. In England, nothing we do makes any sense. That's why we're so vital, and why you're sinking fast, you know what I mean?

**Beau**   Yes, well, I am sure that's a delicious sociological insight, but nonetheless . . .

**Rufus**   Yes! Yes! I heard the Brooklyn!

**Beau**   What?

**Rufus**   When you said "I am sure." Don't you think that's amazing? How did Brooklyn work its way into a Southern accent?

**Beau**   *I don't know!*

**Rufus**   Don't be upset. We had such nice sex. Didn't we? I thought we did . . . I'm sorry. Sorrrry. I talk too much.

*Playfully rests his head against* **Beau***'s chest.*

**Beau** (*stares at him*)   *Law degree?*

**Rufus**   I know, I know, I know, it's so boring. I'm a junior, in the city, mergers and acquisitions, doesn't that phrase just suggest a life . . .

**Beau**   How did you know about Mabel?

**Rufus**   A friend of mine, an older friend, who knows I'm fixated on the middle of the twentieth century, particularly in America, mentioned it when we were at Ralph's . . .

**Beau**   Ralph's?

**Rufus**   Yes.

**Beau**   You saw me there?

**Rufus**   Yes. Playing.

**Beau**   Oh.

**Rufus**    I'd seen you before. You play the piano there every night.

**Beau**    Five nights.

**Rufus**    Oh?

**Beau**    Only five nights. So you knew everything about me when you came over for . . .

**Rufus**    An "assignation."

**Beau**    Indeed.

**Rufus**    Not everything. Just that you accompanied Mabel Mercer in the early sixties. That's all.

**Beau**    You make me feel . . .

**Rufus**    What?

**Beau**    Like trivia.

**Rufus** (*takes his hand and kisses it*)    Sorrry . . .

*Kisses his lips.*

You wouldn't like me if all I had to talk about were mergers and acquisitions. Tell me about Mabel Mercer.

**Beau** *is quiet, a bit lost in the past, a bit discombobulated by the present.*

**Rufus**    Please.

*Pause.*

**Beau**    She sat on a chair and she sang.

**Rufus**    That's it? Come on . . . I really want to know.

**Beau**    You do, don't you?

**Rufus**    Yes, come on.

**Beau**    Well, she sang in a little club. In New York. In the forties and fifties. And sixties. She'd play an engagement at a club for seven or eight years—*years*—and then move on to another club. Usually downstairs. Not that many tables. She was big, I suppose overweight, but that wasn't a consideration, she was beautiful. Regal. She sat with her hands clasped in her lap. She barely moved. And she sang.

**Rufus**    Her voice?

**Beau**    By the early sixties, not much. It had always been a light soprano. It got lighter. But it didn't matter. She made sense of a lyric in a way that no other singer had before. It was the phrasing. And, of course, the pronunciation. Her wonderful British enunciation, emphasizing every vowel. She was born in Stratfordshire. Her mother was English, white, a music-hall performer; her father a black American jazz musician, who did a runner. She was, I suppose, a strange mixture of Harlem and Buckingham Palace.

**Rufus**    The songs?

**Beau**    Ah. The songs. Written for her. Or rescued from a Broadway show that had closed after a short run. They were almost always melancholy and sophisticated and meant something other than what they meant.

**Rufus**    Explain.

**Beau**    This is foolish.

**Rufus**    Go on! I'm loving it!

**Beau**    She was a woman singing about a lover, often a lost lover, a man, of course. But what was unsaid was most of the songs were written by men about lovers, often lost lovers, usually men as well. That was hardly unusual in popular music back then, but somehow, sitting in Mabel's club, surrounded by elegance, her elegance, you were sinking into a different world, and it was a forbidden world, an unspoken world, and yet it *was* being spoken, but in code, although not exactly in code, because it was actually very straightforward, and you came away sad, but exhilarated by that sadness, because it was your life, and you've just been sharing it, although you weren't actually saying anything. If it was a love that daren't speak its name, it was only the name itself that was unspoken, everything else had just been expressed rather eloquently by this rather large, elderly lady with overpronounced vowels sitting in an old, comfortable chair. I suppose she was an acquired taste. But if the virus took you, it was incurable. Some people were immune, of course. But there were no antibodies to Mabel. You can't possibly understand it because it's a world that no longer exists.

**Rufus**    I know. I would have liked to have been there.

**Beau**    No, you wouldn't have.

**Rufus**    But it must have been so much better than now. Wasn't it romantic?

**Beau**    So it seemed. But it wasn't. Everyone was in pain, my dear, everyone was in pain. Someone like Mabel confirmed our misery, and mythologized it, but misery it was. And, as a result, everyone was drunk. We consumed a lot of alcohol in those days. Actually, I need a drink. Can I get you . . .

**Rufus**    I don't drink.

**Beau**    When, later, I discovered the joy of narcotics, I did take a lot of acid at one point. I wonder if this is some kind of flashback. Am I hallucinating you?

**Rufus**    I don't think so. I think I'm real. I want to hear about New Orleans.

**Beau** (*pouring himself a drink*)    I thought I had arranged for a fuck, not an interview.

**Rufus**    I'm just interested in stuff.

**Beau**    I'm not. Stuff's overrated.

**Rufus**    New Orleans.

**Beau**    I left when I was twenty-one. End of story.

**Rufus**    James Baldwin. You knew James Baldwin.

**Beau** *looks at him, amazed.*

**Rufus**   My friend told me.

**Beau**   Does your mind jump around a lot?

**Rufus**   Oh, it does, it does. I'm lower-case bipolar.

**Beau**   Lower-case?

**Rufus**   It's not really serious. But, yes, sometimes my head races.

**Beau**   When I was young, everyone was alcoholic. Now everyone is bipolar. Are you sure you don't want a . . .

**Rufus**   No. My parents drink.

**Beau**   Most parents do.

**Rufus**   Mine drink too much.

**Beau**   Oh. Is that a problem?

**Rufus**   What a silly question.

**Beau**   Unlike yours . . .

**Rufus**   My questions are highly intelligent, and they elicit information. Things I'm interested in, you know what I mean? Aren't you warm?

**Beau**   No.

**Rufus**   Can't we open a window?

**Beau**   I don't like draughts. I catch colds easily.

**Rufus**   You have the heat up.

**Beau** (*irritated*)   Perhaps I do. I'm really sorry.

**Rufus**   But it's so hot. I hate sweating. There's a company gym. I used to go all the time, but now I'm so over it. People just sweat fear there. It's hard to imagine cogs in a wheel sweating, isn't it? How do you stay in shape?

**Beau**   I stretch.

**Rufus**   Do you have a lot of tension at Ralph's? Oh, you probably don't. James Baldwin, come on . . .

**Beau**   Who are you? The FBI? What do you want me to say?

**Rufus**   I don't know. Give me a taste . . .

**Beau**   A taste?

**Rufus**   Of the times.

**Beau**   You know, you're scary.

**Rufus**   Why? Does anyone else you know want to hear about James Baldwin?

**Beau**   Not really.

**Rufus**   Doesn't that make you sad?

*Silence.*

**Beau**   We were friends for a while. Back then. He came to hear Mabel, once. I had only just arrived in New York, but was already her accompanist.

**Rufus**   Did you sleep with him?

**Beau**   A bit.

**Rufus**   What do you mean "a bit"?

**Beau**   He liked to talk, he was, after all, a preacher, so the conversation enveloped me, the conversation fucked me, really, the conversation made me cum. Is that what you want to know? Talking was a defense, of course, he thought he was ugly. He wasn't. He was also, for someone so famously angry, deeply gentle and kind. Much kinder than the other literary lions of the time, who one tended to meet if you were young and good-looking and new to the city; it's amazing the passage we all made around Truman and Tennessee and Gore; especially if you were Southern, like me; but they were all drowning in self-contempt, like almost everyone else was in those days, those days that you so fancy, as I suppose Jimmy was as well, but he was, in keeping with his family calling, a true Christian. Years later, he . . . Well, never mind. I suppose what's important is the knowledge that once upon a distant time, self-hatred made for great literature.

*Lost in thought for a moment, then:*

You know, it might be the proper moment for you to leave.

**Rufus**   Oh. OK.

**Beau**   Wouldn't want you to overheat.

**Rufus**   No.

**Beau**   And I think I've answered a few questions too many.

**Rufus**   Oh. Sorrrry . . .

*Pause.*

**Beau**   Is your name really Rufus?

**Rufus**   Yes. Why would I lie?

**Beau**   I did.

**Rufus**   I worked that out. I didn't think your parents named you "Autumn Leaf." Anyhow, I already knew you were the cocktail pianist from Ralph's, Beauregard; which is, by the way, such an old-fashioned deep-Southern name, only slightly less embarrassing than Autumn Leaf . . .

**Beau**   Thanks.

**Rufus** (*pause*)   Well . . .

**Beau**   What?

**Rufus**   Nothing.

**Beau**   Oh.

**Rufus**   Well, just a thought.

**Beau**    Which is?

**Rufus**    I could stay.

**Rufus** *beams.* **Beau** *looks perplexed.*

*Blackout.*


*Mabel Mercer is heard singing "He Was Too Good to Me" (Richard Rodgers and Lorenz Hart).*


*Lights rise on* **Beau***.*

**Beau**    My last Fat Tuesday. The parades were winding down in The Quarter, the frenzy was about to end, it was over, Mardi Gras was over. Big Al came to see me. Oh yes, we actually did call people things like that then. Big Al. He happened to be my father. Never liked me, though. Preferred Little Al. Little Al was Big Al *melted*. Big Al ran all the gambling tables right outside the city limits. He was, shall we say, *connected* to one of the five or six major Mafia godfathers in the States. Who was actually rather nice. He used to smile at me in a way Big Al never did. Maybe he fancied me. Maybe he just felt sorry for the little faggot, which was exactly the word my father used on that last Fat Tuesday. Faggot, faggot, faggot. I believe it's no longer in currency. Well, Big Al told me that he heard I had been seen in Miss Dixie's—Miss Dixie ran the big gay club on Bourbon Street, across from Jean Lafitte In Exile, the *other* prominent gay emporium. Dixie's had courtyards and staircases and balconies, with lots of little faggots draped around large wicker chairs; I used to like to sit there and play the piano; although I would sometimes nip across the street to the Lafitte, which was much darker and intimate, although there were huge torches, flambeaux, outside, that cast flickering shadows on the walls, shadows that touched down on the now preoccupied little faggots, where my fingers sought more than just piano keys. Of course it was impossible to keep a secret of any kind in The Quarter, so I shouldn't have been so surprised when Big Al said I had been seen patronizing both Miss Dixie's and Jean Lafitte In Exile and that wasn't a good image for the son of a crook. His associates, meaning the Mafia minions, didn't care for faggots, and if I wasn't more cautious I might end up in some sort of cement at the bottom of Lake Pontchartrain, so why didn't I make things simpler for everyone, particularly for Big Al, and probably for Little Al, who I think set the whole thing up and was anxious to inherit the roulette tables, why didn't I make things simpler and just leave town. Go East, he said. It's easier for faggots there. I was always struck by that sentence; I detected a hint of affection or even care. "Go where it's easier." Most fatherly thing he ever said to me. And he put an envelope down, with some money in it, of course. I never saw him again. I did not want to leave. You could not walk down a street in The Quarter without hearing music. And I loved music. And I knew I'd never again see any place quite as beautiful. And I haven't. But cement had no appeal to me, and if there was one truth in a city as elusive as New Orleans, it was that no one there ever made an idle threat, so on the day after Fat Tuesday, on that first day of Lent, I gave up The City That Time Forgot. That was the first occasion on which I left New Orleans.

*Lights up on* **Beau**'s *front room. 2002.* **Beau** *is talking to a video camera, which is being manipulated by* **Rufus**.

**Rufus**    And the second?

**Beau**    A long time later.

**Rufus**    When?

**Beau**    Oh, for God's sake.

*Pause.*

1973. June 25. I don't like this anymore. (*Gestures towards the video camera.*) Put that thingy down. I'm not a movie star. I've gone too far, I think, in my attempts to amuse or please you. You're turning me into "Grey Gardens." The past is dead.

**Rufus** (*smiles*)    The past is sexy.

*Puts the camera down.*

Anyhow—they wouldn't really have killed you, would they?

**Beau**    I suppose it's difficult to understand; these days coming out is something like an unplanned bar mitzvah, but once upon a time, it could end up in cement. Still does, by the way, in half the world. Why are you so fascinated by the past when you care so little about history?

**Rufus** (*smiles*)    Because I'm young.

**Beau**    Increasingly not. You've had a birthday.

**Rufus**    You're right. I'm ancient. I'm going to live my entire life in mergers and acquisitions. My life is so boring, isn't it? I'll never have the kind of adventures you had.

**Beau**    Do you think being disowned by my family is an adventure? *It's not romantic!* What will you do with these tapes?

**Rufus**    I don't know, I don't know, I don't know what I'm going to do with them. It's just a hobby, do you know what I mean? An outlet for my . . .

**Beau**    Demented energy.

**Rufus**    I was going to say curiosity.

**Beau**    You should ask a doctor for some medicine.

**Rufus**    It's all under control. And, anyhow, I like the buzz. And you allow me to have it. That's good. I never had a place to put the buzz before. I have to keep a lid on in the office. I just sit there and worry about chargeable hours and redundancies. I can relax here. Get excited and be cool at the same time.

**Beau**    Because I'm fatherly . . .

**Rufus**    You're not in the least. Come on, let's have a cuddle . . .

**Beau**    Why haven't I met any friends of yours that are your own age?

**Rufus**    How could I talk with someone my own age? Discuss Sugababes? *Sugababes?* When we could be talking about the Andrews Sisters? Don't you realize how hellish everyday conversations are for me? Do you have to be on time tonight?

**Beau**    Yes.

**Rufus**    Why don't you hate *your* job?

**Beau**    It's what I do. I've been a cocktail pianist for half my life.

**Rufus**    Didn't you ever want to be anything else?

**Beau**    Not really.

**Rufus**    You're so sorted.

**Beau**    It happens with . . .

**Rufus**    *Age!!* Don't say it, don't say it. Shouldn't this be the other way around? Shouldn't I be the one who's bothered by . . . The Gap?!

**Beau**    Well, yes, you should be. Look—there are things we have to discuss.

**Rufus**    Uh-oh.

**Beau**    Things we haven't talked about.

**Rufus**    I thought we could just have a quick . . .

**Beau**    Not now, not now . . .

**Rufus**    You don't like me anymore.

**Beau**    I can't bear you.

*Kisses him.*

Look. I more than like you, you know that. And I like this.
I never dreamed I would allow anything like this to happen;
but it happened, you happened, and I let it, and it was easy, I
didn't resist, I even like the fact that you've moved in. Well, I
suppose I didn't have much to say about it, you can be very
pushy. Still . . . And I like going away with you. After all, the
worst thing about being alone is having to put suntan lotion
on your own back. That doesn't have to happen anymore. It's
good.

**Rufus**    Great. Happy ending.

**Beau**    Don't say that.

**Rufus**    Come here . . .

**Beau**    I want you to think about a child.

**Rufus**    Oh my God! You're really getting into this.
Actually, I was going to bring it up someday . . .

**Beau**    Don't even go there. That's not what I meant. I want
you to think about how a child changes in the first twenty
years of their lives.

**Rufus**    What do you mean?

**Beau**    Think how different an infant is than a child of two,
and how different two is from four, and four from seven, and
seven from ten, and ten from, oh God, all the adolescent
years. Every year there's some kind of radical growth. Then,
starting in your twenties, it quiets down, and the changes are
more subtle and sneak up on you. Then in old age, it becomes
the opposite of childhood. The decline, year to year, accelerates.
I'm sixty-two now. If I make it to seventy I'll be very different.
And then seventy-five . . . And then . . .

**Rufus**    Yes, yes, I get it . . .

**Beau**    Right now you're not repelled by my flesh, but at
some point you will be . . .

**Rufus**    (*nuzzling his neck*)    Never, never, never . . .

**Beau**    Stop it! You will be. The aches, the pains, the illnesses, the qvetching, the forgetting, the marbles scattering in every direction . . . I don't want you to wake up one day at thirty-five and realize that your major obsession has become my prostate . . .

**Rufus**    I think this is a ridiculous thing to discuss . . .

**Beau**    I don't want to steal your youth. Do you understand? I don't want you to have to take care of me. At some point you're going to have to let me go. You're going to have to live your own life.

**Rufus**    We'll cross that . . .

**Beau**    OK, I've said it, it's out there, it's on the table, it won't go away. That's the future. Now let's deal with the present. I'll understand if you want to see other people . . .

**Rufus**    What? You mean . . .

**Beau**    Yes, sleep with other people. Closer to your own age.

**Rufus**    Ugh!! You won't be jealous?

**Beau**    Absolutely not. Not under these circumstances. You mustn't stop being young.

**Rufus**    Why would I see anyone else?

**Beau**    You might suddenly fancy a single chin.

**Rufus**    Nonsense. You keep me calm.

**Beau**    Maybe you shouldn't be calm. Maybe you should be excited.

**Rufus**    That's not good for my condition.

**Beau**    So I'm like a pill?

**Rufus** ( *jumps up and opens a window*)    I'd only be attracted to someone else if they liked fresh air.

**Beau**    Well, maybe you'll meet someone who does.

**Rufus**    Why are you trying to get rid of me?

**Beau**    I'm simply pointing out . . .

**Rufus**    You *are* trying to get rid of me. I scare you.

**Beau**    Don't be ridiculous.

**Rufus**    You don't think it's possible to be happy!!

**Beau**    Oh, that's absurd. What's happy?

**Rufus**    Not being at the office is happy. Not being off my face in some club is happy. Not going back to Gaydar is happy. Not being in my parents' house is happy. Not listening to their drunken arguments is *very* happy, especially when they're arguing about me. My family always considered me a freak, you know, and not simply because I was gay—coming out was not a bar mitzvah, by the way, it was more like a bris—look it up!—but because my mind wandered and I didn't like masculine stuff like football or even feminine stuff like needlepoint, I wasn't in a category, I was never in a category, do you know what I mean, I was neither exactly normal, nor sufficiently strange, like they would have been alright if I was gay*er*, but instead I was just queer, without the sexual connotation; I would, for instance, go to exhibitions of antique church organs, just think about *that*; actually, I just thought I was eccentric, which was once a national trait, aren't the British meant to be eccentric, when did all that die away, when did eccentric become neurotic, and anyhow, happy is a totally illogical concept, except it's not, it's something, when I'm with you I feel *something*, and that something is both heated and ordinary at the same time, and I feel like it's OK for me to actually be here, I mean *here*, on this planet, that I'm not totally from Mars, and well, I don't know, we can argue about the meaning of the word happiness, and clearly I don't understand the meaning of the word, but whatever, who cares, I have a right to it.

*Pause.*

**Beau**    I have to let that sink in.

**Rufus**    Where are you going?

**Beau**    I need some air.

**Rufus**    Good! I'll open a window.

**Beau**    This is all too fast. And I just gave in, gave in, too easily. I don't like what's ahead.

**Rufus**    Why do you think everything ends badly?

**Beau**    Because it always does.

*He leaves.*

*Blackout.*


*Lights up on* **Beau***, talking for the video camera..*

**Beau**    It's 1984 and I'm in Paris, playing at a club there, and I meet George. I had promised myself that I would never again have a relationship, not after Kip. I'm not going to talk about Kip, by the way. There's a good few years of my life that are not going on tape. George was utterly mad. He had a manic energy, rather like yours, clearly I'm attracted to that. He had a small troupe of actors, Canadian mostly, George was Canadian, and each summer they toured a Greek play— to Greece! They took it to the Greek islands, where the very last thing the sun-worshipping, beer-guzzling, sex-searching tourists needed was a rather bad group of Canadian amateurs performing Euripides. The entire project was so bizarre it rather enchanted the Greeks. The actors themselves weren't paid, they just had the opportunity to spend a summer in Greece. George did all the translations himself, and directed, and acted a major role in each play. It was hard to say no to him, particularly if the request was excessively outlandish. He wasn't particularly attractive, but he burned energy, and energy can be as sexually provocative as beauty or power. He asked me to come along and play music for them. I pointed

out that a piano wasn't exactly portable and for that reason
not a feature of travelling players. He said, well, drums then,
anyone can play drums. And I said OK. You see, I give in,
and it's a mistake, it's a weakness, I don't know whether it's
passivity or a misguided optimism, perhaps they're the same
thing. Maybe it was just passion. I had forsworn passion after
Kip. But George was undeniable. I knew it would end badly,
because that was just simply the way it was with our lot, but
that optimistic passivity just pushed me over the bridge and
into the water once again. And so we were a couple. In the
winter, George was a waiter in a decent Parisian restaurant
and I played piano in a decent Parisian club. In the summer
we were off to Skiros and Hydra and Paros and even
Mykonos with an ill-spoken *Iphigenia* or an underpowered
*Oedipus*. We made uncomfortable love on innumerable
beaches, which happened to also serve as our living quarters.
We put up with tantrums from drunken Canadian thespians
and outraged classical scholars and avaricious villagers, and
each summer George would hatch another cockeyed plan for
another tour of another play, blissfully unaware that
somewhere in space, Euripides was begging for mercy. And
then, one summer, George's magnificent energy began to
flag. Flag, falter, fail. I did not live in a bubble, I recognized
the signs of the one subject we tried to avoid, and it was
indeed a bit easier to avoid in Paris or Greece than it was in
America, but still one saw skeletal figures on the beach at
Mykonos or on the Rue Jacob, walking at a tender pace when
once they strode; faces, made to be covered with kisses, now
covered with huge black sores; eyes, once the deepest blue,
now gaping holes staring into an abyss that had no name.
Although there was a name, of course there was a name, but
George never wanted to speak it. I thought I would never
return to America, but that's where the medical community
was most organized, and somehow I talked him into
returning with me.

New York had turned into an animated graveyard. Gays
were pilloried and despised whilst at the same time being

ignored, which was rather a hat trick if you ask me; and most
of all, they were dying. Dying, and yet here's the strange
thing, coming alive at the same time. Alive with anger. And
making themselves known. Speaking out. There were
organizations, some of them loud, some of them conciliatory,
but all serving a purpose. And in the midst of the chaos stood
a modern Jeremiah or Ezekial, a raging Old Testament
prophet, named Larry Kramer, spewing forth curses and
truths that no one, not even his friends, wanted to hear, but
which all, alas, came to pass. I knew him from the early days;
he told me where to take George. George could no longer be
in active denial; there were too many others, looking gaunt
and broken, surrounding him in the city, so he cloaked
himself in a more attractive denial; he was sick, that was true,
but he would beat it. It wasn't going to get *him*. He had, alas,
forgotten all the basic tenets of Greek tragedy; certainly he no
longer worshipped inevitability. He saw doctors. He took
useless medicine. He would become ill with a weird malady,
then recover, then be struck down again by something
equally bizarre. He didn't have illnesses, he had plagues.
We went to an organization that offered emotional help and
therapy. His councilor was a pencil-thin, middle-aged
woman, a sparrow in Chanel, adorned in diamonds and
pearls, with birdcage hair, who had clearly stepped out of the
pages of the Social Register. Her name was Judy Peabody, and
she was *a* Peabody, which was an odd thought because she
had also, clearly, been sent by God. This delicate bird picked
up my George with her almost invisible wrist and enveloped
him with love; as indeed she did with hundreds of other
young, frightened men. This unmotherly woman effortlessly
filled a maternal role that was otherwise vacant. At some
point she had stopped going to society balls and glittering
benefits and devoted herself to dying young men for no
reason other than *she had to*. George was able to tell her things
he couldn't tell me, express terrors he kept from my ears. My
ears, as it happened, were burning with nightmarish
sentences. Tests had established that I had somehow escaped
the virus, this being a disease with a profound sense of irony,

but there were no hospital beds for survivors, no nurses for a bleeding soul, and I literally couldn't catch my breath and one morning I ran to Port Authority and went to the ticket window and realized I didn't know where to go. So I returned to George and waited for the end, and it obliged fairly soon, and he died in my arms. And now George is a memory only, that awkward little talent that made the world a stranger place, gone; there are no longer wandering troupes of bad Canadian actors mangling *Agamemnon* on Corfu, and it's difficult to explain what a profound loss that is. I went back to Paris, but Paris was itself in mourning, for its own glorious past; so I came to London, where it is possible to simply exist, exist with a minimum of fuss, where the past seems part of today, and today has a foot in the future, and you can accommodate your numbness into a daily pattern of living. And so I was until I met you.

*Lights up on* **Beau**'s *front room. 2004.* **Rufus** *is lying on the couch, covered by blankets.*

**Beau**   They phoned again.

**Rufus** *doesn't reply.*

**Beau**   The office phoned again.

**Rufus** *doesn't reply.*

**Beau**   I said you had a fever.

**Rufus** (*slowly*)   Go away.

**Beau** *considers for a moment, then sits down by the couch.*

**Beau**   No. I'm not going to do that.

**Rufus**   Leave me alone.

**Beau**   I'm not going to leave you.

**Rufus**   I can't breathe. Open the window.

**Beau** *gets up and opens the window.*

**Beau**    There.

**Rufus**    I'm cold.

**Beau**    Right.

*He closes the window.*

There. Won't you be more comfortable in the bedroom?

**Rufus**    I can't move.

**Beau**    OK.

**Rufus**    Go away.

**Beau**    No.

**Rufus**    There's a fog.

**Beau**    Where?

**Rufus**    All over. Sorryyyyy. I'm rubbish, I know it. I shouldn't be doing this to you. Can't help it. I warned you. I get depressed.

**Beau**    *Depressed??!!*

**Rufus**    I crash. I warned you. Get rid of me.

**Beau**    No.

**Rufus**    Leave me alone.

**Beau**    No.

**Rufus**    I'm useless.

**Beau**    No.

**Rufus**    You don't understand.

**Beau**    No.

**Rufus**    You *can't* understand.

**Beau**    That doesn't matter.

**Rufus**    You're not a part of this.

**Beau**   I want to be.

**Rufus**   You can't. You can't. Just pack your things and go.

**Beau**   I can't pack my things; it's my flat.

**Rufus**   I don't care. Go anyhow.

**Beau**   I'm not going anywhere.

**Rufus**   You're a coward.

**Beau**   If you say so.

**Rufus**   I have no colour.

**Beau**   That's not true.

**Rufus**   It's so dark.

**Beau**   Where?

**Rufus**   Everywhere.

**Beau**   I have a torch.

**Rufus**   I can't carry a tune.

**Beau**   So what?

**Rufus**   I don't want to take off my shirt.

**Beau**   You're not wearing a shirt.

**Rufus**   I want to sleep.

**Beau**   Then I think you should. Sleep. Sooner or later, you'll get bored being depressed. Sooner or later, you'll swing back up again. And you'll be all right again. I'll just be here, nearby. I won't say anything. I won't disturb you. But I'll be here. Here.

Alright?

**Rufus** *doesn't reply. He just stares into space.*

**Beau**   Alright.

*Blackout.*

*Mabel Mercer is heard singing "Lonely Little Boy" (Otis Gilmer Clements, Jr).*


*Lights rise on the front room. 2006.* **Beau** *and* **Rufus** *are sitting on the sofa, watching a DVD. Ballet music can be heard. They are eating popcorn.*

**Rufus**    I'm putting all your tapes onto a disc.

**Beau**    I would think they might sell for a fortune.

**Rufus**    We'll be able to do something with them . . . Someday I'll figure it out . . . I wish you played chess . . . I would love to play chess with you . . .

**Beau**    Why?

**Rufus**    So I can *outwit* you.

**Beau** (*laughs*)    You probably would. Anyhow, you don't play chess.

**Rufus**    No, but I'd learn.

(*Focusing back on the screen.*) The gestures are too big.

**Beau**    What do you mean?

**Rufus**    Overdramatic.

**Beau**    They're meant for a big stage, not for film.

**Rufus**    I wish I saw them live. That must have been a golden era.

**Beau**    You say that about every time except now . . . Have some more.

*Hands him the popcorn.*

**Rufus**    Thanks. I shouldn't have so much. I'll get huge. Like everyone else at the firm. Why do lawyers put on weight? Anyhow, I even like the sound of their names: Nureyev and

Fonteyn. They go together so well. Were they the perfect partnership?

**Beau**   There's no such thing, is there? I actually preferred it when he danced with Lynn Seymour.

**Rufus**   Who was she?

**Beau**   She was a . . . You don't want to hear this.

**Rufus**   Of course I do. This is great.

**Beau**   No, it's not.

**Rufus**   But you know that's what I want to hear. I want to *know*. Tell me more. Especially about partnerships. Do you think we're perfect partners?

**Beau**   We're very odd ones.

**Rufus**   Odd, but nice, don't you think?

*A silence.*

Come on—say it.

**Beau** (*smiles*)   Yes. Nice.

**Rufus**   There, that wasn't too difficult, was it? This is my idea of perfection. Popcorn. A DVD. And you.

**Beau** (*laughs*)   *Who are you?*

*Kisses* **Rufus**.

**Beau**   I don't care. I don't care how strange you are.

*Pause.*

You're right. This is sort of a bonkers stab at perfection.

**Rufus**   Oh good. So then—why don't we become civil?

**Beau**   What do you mean?

**Rufus**   A civil partnership.

**Beau**   Don't be ridiculous.

**Rufus**   Well, why not? That way I can get all your money.

**Beau**   Very funny.

**Rufus**   Well, it's an official stamp. It kind of makes us real. Under the law.

**Beau**   A new law. Who knows if it will take?

**Rufus**   It will. Law is something I know about.

**Beau**   But not something you like to talk about.

**Rufus**   This is an exception. An important exception.

**Beau**   You're being childish.

**Rufus**   No. For once, I'm not.

*He looks at* **Beau**. *He moves away from the sofa.*

**Rufus**   If you analyze what just happened, I proposed . . .

**Beau**   No, you didn't; you just asked one of your irritating questions.

**Rufus**   Oh? Is that what it was?

*Pause.*

Still—the question stands. Why not?

**Beau**   Why not? Who ever said we were meant to be *legal*? We're supposed to be outlaws; we're supposed to be inventing new rules, not imitating all the old conventions, not going backwards . . . When did you suddenly become so boring? Anyway, why are the British the only people in the world who presume that a partnership can be civil?

**Rufus**   What is it—do you think someday what we have will evaporate, it will just be a memory, like Nureyev dancing?

**Beau**   Let's not talk about this.

**Rufus**   I *am* your partner. In every way. You know that.

**Beau**   Sure. Have some more . . .

*He holds out the popcorn.* **Rufus** *looks at him.*

**Rufus** (*quietly*)    I was serious.

**Beau** *continues to offer the popcorn.* **Rufus** *closes his eyes for a second, then opens them, and walks toward the outstretched popcorn.*

*Blackout.*

*Lights up on* **Beau**.

**Beau**    Sam told me. About the good times. About the old days meeting at the Astor Bar in New York. The Astor was a legendary hotel near Times Square, and one entire side of the oval bar was reserved for gay men, discreet gay men, of course, and usually soldiers. This was World War Two and the goings-on at the Astor Bar were referred to as "wartime ambience." Sailors, soldiers, marines even, could make contact there. Gay life, always secret and furtive and forbidden, blossomed during the war. The American army needed bodies, they weren't in a position to overtly discriminate. Young men, whose inner life had always been hidden, suddenly were put in contact with other young men whose inner life had always been hidden. The results were combustible. So Sam said. He remembered going with another soldier to a YMCA and taking a room and having sex, and after sex, his friend, who was rural, from someplace in the Dakotas, I think, was so full of joy, he started singing a childhood nursery rhyme.

Row, row, row your boat
Gently down the stream
Merrily, merrily, merrily, merrily
Life is but a dream.

The walls, of course, were paper thin, and suddenly from another room, he heard another soldier's voice, joining in, a very deep baritone, and then from another room, another voice, and, and then the entire Young Men's Christian Association, including Sam, seemed to be singing, but not just singing, *harmonizing,* everyone remembering their own childhood and the pain of it, and now suddenly this sense of release:

> Row, row, row your boat
> Gently down the stream
> Merrily, merrily, merrily, merrily
> Life is but a dream.

Sam said that was the happiest moment of his life.

I met Sam in Rio. I would occasionally stop playing for Mabel, and accept jobs in other cities. There was a lazy moon over a capricious sea, and everyone was drop dead beautiful, and the shanty towns were off, off, somewhere in the haze. Sam was off, off somewhere in a haze too. He used to show up at the club, always drunk, always miserable. He said he was a beachcomber, but I doubt it, I'm certain he was following shadier pursuits. But if he had had a former self, he was now a shadow of it. When he realized I was a "fruit," his word, he opened up. He said there were things he wanted me to know. About the good times. He said if we didn't tell others of our kind, it would all be lost. He said the war was a golden time, a somewhat narrow view, I imagine, for the millions consigned to ovens. He said you could be queer, and meet other queers, and fuck other queers, and no one minded, and, indeed, everyone thought the world had changed. But then, of course, as soon as the war ended, everything tightened, and it was worse than before, and people were hounded and persecuted, and the Astor Bar had you arrested if you so much as looked at another man inappropriately, and McCarthyism ruled the waves, and Sam, himself, who had been something of a hero, a Purple Heart evidently for rescuing a platoon, and who had been planning on medical school after the war, just drifted, and found himself, twenty some years later, a drunken wreck in Rio de Janiero. It's an old war story. Sam's lesson, the one he was desperate to impart, was that the good times are fleeting. One day they disappear, and you never know they had existed to begin with. He kept saying *you have to know about these things.* Well, perhaps that justifies these videos. And perhaps I shouldn't make fun of your bizarre curiosity. Alright, I've just made a pact with myself, to excuse your thirst for the past. Are you happy?

*Lights rise on* **Beau**'s *front room. 2008.* **Beau** *is drinking a cup of hot chocolate.* **Rufus** *stands over him.*

**Rufus**   It's your favourite.

**Beau**   Hot chocolate. Yes.

**Rufus**   Good.

**Beau**   But why?

**Rufus**   What do you mean?

**Beau**   I arrive home from a boring evening tinkling the keys, and you have a delicious cup of Belgian hot chocolate waiting for me. Must mean something.

**Rufus**   No. Nothing at all.

**Beau**   This is almost as fine as the extra-thick hot chocolate that's made by a machine, the kind you can eat with a spoon; there was a café in Rome that I used to patronize that . . . Have I told you this?

**Rufus**   Yes.

**Beau**   Many times?

**Rufus**   Yes.

**Beau**   Oh dear.

*Pause.*

You seem subdued.

**Rufus**   No.

**Beau**   You're not about to plunge into a depression, are you? You promised you'd tell me if you felt any warning signs.

**Rufus**    No. I haven't been low in almost a year.

**Beau**    I really wish you'd take medicine.

**Rufus**    No. End of conversation.

**Beau**    What *is* the conversation?

**Rufus**    What do you mean?

**Beau**    What's the hot chocolate about, then?

**Rufus**    Nothing. Just a warm way to end the evening.
That's all.

*Sits down, picks up a book, starts to read, then looks up.*

I thought it would be a treat.

*Sitarts to read again, then looks up again.*

Memories of a café in Rome.

*Starts to read, then looks up again.*

Actually . . .

*Starts to read, then looks up again.*

But I must learn to make it thicker, so you really *can* eat it
with a spoon.

*Starts to read, then looks up again.*

I've met somebody. I'm seeing somebody.

*Returns to the book.*

*Pause.*

**Beau**    What are you reading?

**Rufus**    Germaine Greer.

**Beau**    Well, at least she's English . . .

**Rufus**    Australian. Didn't you hear what I said?

**Beau**    Yes.

**Rufus**   And . . . ?

**Beau**   I'm very tired.

**Rufus**   I was so nervous. I didn't know how to tell you. I'm embarrassed. I feel terrible. I love you.

**Beau**   Really, but you just said . . .

**Rufus**   I can love more than one person. There's room in me.

**Beau**   Ah, so you're in love with this person that you're "seeing"?

**Rufus**   I don't know yet.

**Beau**   *Yet?*

**Rufus**   Yet. Are you upset?

**Beau**   No, why would I be upset?

**Rufus**   You said that's what you wanted.

**Beau**   I know.

**Rufus**   You wanted me to see other people.

**Beau**   I know.

**Rufus**   So I listened to you.

**Beau**   I'm tired. I'm going to bed now . . .

**Rufus**   You're *really* upset!

**Beau**   Of course I'm *really* upset.

**Rufus**   But you said . . .

**Beau**   I was *lying*! I don't wish to discuss it.

**Rufus**   You were happy to talk about it *before* it happened, *in anticipation* of it happening, why not now that it has?

**Beau**   Don't force me to be logical.

**Rufus**   I don't believe you were lying.

**Beau**    OK, I thought I was telling the truth. But I wasn't, was I?

**Rufus**    But you've been expecting this.

**Beau**    I'm expecting to die too; it doesn't mean I want it to happen. Although at the moment, that's debatable. Oh look, this is how everything ends, I've always told you that, there is no hope, you know, not for two guys, ever . . . Of course you found somebody else, I told you what would happen to me, look at the flesh under my elbows, have you seen the flesh under my elbows, it's absolutely obvious, if you have a daddy fixation, give it enough time, and daddy turns into grandad, and where does that get you, where does that get anyone, of course this happened, of course. I'm not upset. I'm very happy for you. It's what I wanted. *How could you do this?* I didn't want to rob you of your youth, you know that. My God, I hope he's the same age.

**Rufus**    Oh please. Of course not.

**Beau**    Figures.

**Rufus**    Younger.

**Beau**    *Younger?*

**Rufus**    Seven years younger.

**Beau**    Seven?! That's obscene!

**Rufus**    Don't be ridiculous; he's twenty-eight, I'm thirty five, as gaps go it's . . .

**Beau**    OK, OK. Does he have a profession?

**Rufus**    He's a performing artist.

**Beau**    What's that?

**Rufus**    A performing artist.

**Beau**    Is he a performer or an artist?

**Rufus**    Both, I guess.

**Beau**    Is he one of those people who urinates on stage?

**Rufus**    Beau!

**Beau**    Or pulls a loo brush out of his bum.

**Rufus**    A cell phone, actually.

**Beau**    What?

**Rufus**    He pulls a cell phone out . . .

**Beau**    I don't wanna hear. Is it ringing?

**Rufus**    Of course. What would be the point otherwise?
I thought you'd be pleased for me, you know what I mean?

**Beau**    I am pleased for you. No—honestly—I am. You've
found somebody younger, that's as it should be, somebody
who bites off chicken heads on a stage, or whatever; I have to
say, it sounds rather odd . . .

**Rufus**    Well, I can't explain him any more than I can
explain you. My tastes are eccentric.

**Beau**    It's amazing how sometimes you get caught in a trap.
Despite everything your life has told you, you actually think,
perhaps it's better now, *better,* and then, of course, it isn't. I'm
going to bed.

**Rufus**    Don't.

*Goes to him and kisses him.*

**Beau**    What are you doing?

**Rufus**    Don't.

**Beau**    You're being unfaithful to . . .

**Rufus**    Harry.

**Beau** (*grimaces*)    Harry.

**Rufus**    He knows how I feel about you. I'm just confused.

**Beau**    Your lips taste of hot chocolate.

**Rufus**    I know. It's your favourite.

**Beau**    I just wanted to sit in my room; well, play the piano every night and make a living, and then come home and sit in my room, and read, and watch a little telly, and play charades with my friends, and occasionally have an "assignation" that was pleasant but meaningless, and if I ever became depressed, simply eat a lot of ice cream, and then sit in my room some more, and not have any more *damage*, and then I allowed myself, allowed myself, with no resistance at all, to open a door and step into an empty hole, like the shaft of a lift, just plunge down, again, again, into an abyss, I always hated that word, it was very popular in the sixties, very existential, people were always staring into an abyss, and I never knew what it meant, but I do now, it means nothing, staring into *nothing* . . . when, actually, I could have been sitting in my room, making my own hot chocolate . . .

**Rufus**    I love you . . .

*Kisses him again.*

**Beau**    But not enough . . .

**Rufus** (*unbuttons* **Beau***'s shirt*)    I want you . . .

**Rufus** *starts to make love to* **Beau***.*

**Beau**    Oh shit, shit, shit, shit . . .

*Blackout.*


*Mabel Mercer is heard singing "Isn't He Adorable?" (Cy Coleman-Joseph McCarthy).*

*Lights up on the front room. 2010.* **Rufus***' belongings have been packed in boxes, but most of them have now been removed; only a few remain. He sits on one of them, and looks, ruefully, at* **Beau***.*

**Rufus**    I reckon that's everything.

**Beau**    Umm . . .

**Rufus**    I'm not going to be far away . . .

**Beau**    I know . . .

**Rufus**    If you need anything, just pick up the phone . . .

**Beau**    Stop it.

**Rufus**    Stop what?

**Beau**    Stop treating me like a senior citizen.

**Rufus**    I'm not . . .

**Beau**    Patronizing me . . .

**Rufus**    I'm not . . .

**Beau**    It's not as if I haven't lived alone before . . .

**Rufus**    Yes, I know, but . . .

**Beau**    I have most of my life . . .

**Rufus**    Yes, I'm very aware of . . .

**Beau**    And I prefer it that way.

**Rufus**    I'm certain you do . . .

**Beau**    It will be a relief . . .

**Rufus**    Good!

**Beau**    You're making a boring assumption that I'm upset or that I'm going to be upset whereas the truth is I'm not the *slightest—bit—upset* . . .

**Harry** *comes in. He is twenty-nine. He wears a T-shirt; his arms are covered in tattoos.*

**Harry**    Anything else?

**Rufus**    Just these.

**Harry**    OK. Jesus, don't you get hot in here?

**Rufus**    He doesn't notice.

**Harry**   It's boiling.

**Rufus**   He's American.

**Harry** *takes the boxes and leaves.*

*Silence.*

*Then:*

**Beau**   I still can't get over the tattoos.

**Rufus**   Don't start.

**Beau**   It's just not you, it's so *contemporary*.

**Rufus**   Tattoos are anything but contemporary. Winston Churchill had an anchor tattooed on his right arm, and his mother had a discreet little snake on her wrist. George Orwell had the knuckles on one hand covered with blue dots. And George V had a dragon . . .

**Beau**   Alright, alright, I'm sorry I said anything . . .

**Rufus**   It's rumoured that Queen Victoria had a very small tattoo someplace private . . . (*Stops.*) Sorry. Search engine.

**Beau**   I'm going to miss you.

**Rufus**   We're only twenty minutes away. In London, that's virtually next door.

**Beau**   You'll be all right?

**Rufus**   Why wouldn't I be? You have grown to like Harry, haven't you?

**Beau**   Yes, of course, it's simply that I worry about his history . . .

**Rufus**   What do you mean?

**Beau**   Crystal meth . . .

**Rufus**   That's just a rite of passage, in a Russian roulette kind of way. I knew it was a mistake telling you. Just because

I never did that stuff, doesn't mean everyone else hasn't. Anyhow, he's been clean for five years.

**Beau**   Yes, but . . .

**Rufus**   When did you start playing an age-appropriate role? You never believed me when I said I didn't want a daddy; well, I didn't, and I certainly don't want one now, you know what I mean?

**Harry** *returns.*

**Harry**   Car's packed.

**Beau**   You better be off, then.

**Harry** (*to* **Beau**)   You're limping.

**Beau**   Hip hurts.

**Harry**   Have you seen a doctor?

**Beau**   No.

**Harry**   You should.

**Beau**   Maybe.

**Harry** (*to* **Rufus**)   Make him see a doctor.

**Beau** (*mimics* **Harry**)   "Make him see a doctor." (*To* **Rufus**.) Oh, honey, if you didn't want a daddy before, I think you may have one now.

**Harry** (*puts his arms around* **Rufus**)   Yeah, I want to be a father!

**Rufus**   Later.

**Harry** (*to* **Beau**)   So—I've been watching your videos. It's like Morocco. You know, like in Marrakech. The old storytellers, sitting in the square . . .

**Beau**   I can't tell you how that's picked up my spirits . . .

**Harry**   Did I say something wrong? I have to be so careful with you.

**Beau**    No, it's fine, Harry. An old storyteller.

**Harry**    It's a great tradition. You need to preserve stories, don't you? I tried to do a bit in my act, relating to the past, you know, but I can't make it work, not really. Oh, I am taking your advice. I'm doing a gig where I'm just singing. I mean, really, really radical. That's a form of storytelling, isn't it?

**Beau**    It is. Of course, then you'll be a singer, not a performing artist.

**Harry** (*irritated*)    I'll be whatever I want to call it. (*To* **Rufus**.) Let's go, then.

**Rufus**    Yeah. I'll come by Wednesday afternoon.

**Beau**    You don't have to.

**Rufus**    Oh, for Christ's sake. I'll come by Wednesday afternoon!

*He kisses* **Beau** *and leaves, followed by* **Harry**. **Beau** *looks around the flat, which is now back to where it started. He walks to the fridge, takes out a container of ice cream and a spoon, and starts to eat from it. He begins to weep.*

*Blackout.*

*Lights rise on* **Harry**. *He is provocatively dressed. He sings "The Man I Love" (George and Ira Gershwin).*

*Lights rise on the front room. 2013. There is fumbling at the front door, then a key opens it, and* **Harry** *helps a limping* **Beau** *into the room.*

**Harry**    Careful . . .

**Beau**    I'm alright, I'm alright . . .

**Harry**    Don't overdo.

**Beau**    Who ever thought I'd be fashionable?

**Harry**    You're not.

**Beau**    I am. I have the chicest accessory on the market, a new hip.

**Harry**    Don't worry, they'll go out soon . . .

**Beau**    Like bell bottom trousers?

**Harry**    What are they?

**Beau**    Not important.

**Harry**    I'll pick you up tomorrow to take you to physio.

**Beau**    Won't you be rehearsing?

**Harry**    I'm flexible.

**Rufus** *enters.*

**Rufus**    Sorrrry . . . if you take any time off, the office makes you feel like you've committed the kind of crime we're mandated to defend . . . How's the cripple?

**Beau**    In terrific nick.

**Rufus**    Good.

**Beau**    Best doctor in the world.

**Rufus**    Well, that's her reputation.

**Beau**    And we never once mentioned that she had her gender realigned.

**Rufus**    You just did.

**Beau**    I know. But I'm moved by that. If nothing else, it means she understands pain, and that's a doctor you can trust.

**Harry**    OK, I'm off.

**Rufus** (*mouths to* **Harry**. **Beau** *can't see*)    Did you tell him?

**Harry**    That's your job.

**Rufus** *frowns.* **Harry** *kisses* **Beau** *on the cheek.*

**Harry** (*to* **Beau**)    See you tomorrow, killer.

**Harry** *leaves.* **Beau** *is now seated comfortably.*

**Rufus**    Do you need anything?

**Beau**    Don't ask leading questions.

**Rufus**    'Cause I have to run off.

**Beau** (*takes his hand*)    I'm fine. Thanks.

**Rufus**    Oh yeah. There is something I should mention.

**Beau**    Which is?

**Rufus**    We're getting married.

**Beau**    This is so sudden.

**Rufus**    Harry and me.

**Beau**    Ah.

**Rufus**    In August.

**Beau**    Yes, a good time . . .

**Rufus**    Will you give me away?

**Beau**    Haven't I already done so?

**Rufus**    I mean, legally. Will you be my best man?

**Beau**    I never thought I would say this, it's not a word I
regularly use, but . . . *gosh*!

**Rufus**    It's what I'd like.

**Beau**    And Harry?

**Rufus**    He was the first to suggest it.

**Beau**    Marriage . . .

**Rufus**  I know, I know, I know that worries you. I proposed to *you* once, remember? You didn't take it seriously. That decimated me, actually. I mean—I *proposed* to you, Beau.

*A long pause.*

**Beau**  I think I was afraid.

**Rufus**  Of what?

**Beau**  Marrying you.

**Rufus**  Why?

**Beau**  Because if we got married I knew . . .

**Rufus**  Knew what?

**Beau**  That we'd get divorced.

**Rufus**  *What?*

**Beau**  The lawyers, the court case, the settlement, the humiliation, the awful racking heartache . . .

**Rufus**  What are you talking about?

**Beau**  It's what I've been telling you for years . . . There are no happy endings.

**Rufus**  So you made it happen.

**Beau**  What happen?

**Rufus**  Your fantasy, you made it come true. You had to prove you were right. You had to prove you couldn't be happy. Congratulations.

**Beau**  What kind of future would you have had anyhow— with someone my age?

**Rufus**  Well, I wasn't blind. I assumed someday I'd be a widow. People treat you really well. I mean, that's some kind of future. It's an identity. A place. It says, at least for a time, I was loved. I mean, what's the point of being loved if no one knows about it? Isn't that why people get married?

**Beau**    Did anyone ever tell you you're very strange?

**Rufus**    I'm just me. Anyhow, water under whatever . . . And if you had said yes, I wouldn't be marrying Harry, and having a child . . .

**Beau**    *A child?*

**Rufus**    It's on our to-do list.

**Beau**    I see.

**Rufus**    Look, just think about it, will you?

**Beau**    OK.

**Rufus**    Have to run . . .

**Beau**    Wait.

**Rufus**    What?

**Beau**    I don't even have to consider it.

**Rufus**    Really.

**Beau**    I'll do it.

**Rufus**    Great! (*Embraces* **Beau**.) *Thank you.*

**Beau**    With one condition.

**Rufus**    Condition?

**Beau**    You have to go to your doctor and start taking the meds.

**Rufus**    What does one have to do with the other?

**Beau**    Everything. How long do you think Harry will put up with the lows?

**Rufus**    But you know how I love . . .

**Beau**    The highs, yeah. The buzz. Well, I suppose growing up is giving up a bit of the buzz.

**Rufus**    But I'm perfectly . . .

**Beau**    No, you're not. Life *homogenizes*, that's just the way it is. I think you're crazy to want a child. But if you do, do you honestly want your child to grow up with a manic-depressive parent, think about those words, forget bipolar, which sounds Alaskan, *manic—depressive*! OK, OK, OK, I admit, I was attracted to damage. But children aren't; unless they have no choice. You want to do that to a kid? No medicine, no me, simple as that.

**Rufus**    Shit.

**Beau**    Indeed.

**Rufus**    I'll have to think about it.

**Beau**    You do that.

**Rufus** *looks at* **Beau**. *A silence. Blackout.*


*Lights rise on* **Beau**.

**Beau**    I think it's finally time to tell you about Kip. I don't know if I loved Kip more than anyone else, who ever knows those things, and they're not quantifiable anyhow, but I loved him *first*, and that's something we all romanticize, isn't it? I met Kip in San Francisco, in 1970. I had dropped out of New York; the world of placid nightclub songs had lost its appeal; I abandoned Mabel for the sounds of Janis Joplin and Gracie Slick. I was able to work as a sessions man. It was a good period. Especially when Kip entered my life. He was smart and sassy and sexy and, like I say, for the first time in my life, I was genuinely in love. He was also a hippie which was always a misguided name, because, really, he had no hips; but waist-length hair, that he constantly flicked, and washed, and obsessed over, probably with foreboding, as it was the kind of hair that disappears in middle age. Kip was sort of *pre*-queer. He was an activist when very few existed; Stonewall had occurred a year before, but its influence barely registered. He had become obsessed with Jean Malin, who was a pansy entertainer in 1930s New York. Not quite a drag queen,

Malin wore men's clothing but talked like a woman; he was
built like a truck driver, and could deal with hecklers with
either his wit or his knuckles; he appeared everywhere from
dark, subterranean venues to swank, uptown nightclubs; he
was, come to think of it, a performing artist. (Nothing, Harry,
is new; it's all been done before; just a bit differently.) Malin
died young in an automobile accident, but Kip was convinced
that in his openness, and in his gender-bending and blending,
he was a hero before his time. So he haunted libraries to find
newspaper clippings and spoke to punters who had seen
Malin perform, and took copious notes, which he intended to
someday compile into a book.


But first he thought I should go back to New Orleans. Just for
a visit, but back nonetheless. Kip thought it would be a good
idea for my . . . what . . . my soul? And anyhow, he always
wanted to see the city. So we returned to the Big Easy. I was
able to slip into town unnoticed. Miss Dixie's and Jean Lafitte
In Exile were still popular, and I thought it would be fun to
visit them with Kip, but Kip, who knew people everywhere,
had some friends who were getting together for a drink at a
gay bar in The Quarter and asked us to join them; so we
found ourselves in the Upstairs Lounge on Chartres Street.
The Upstairs was new to me, really just a few rooms on the
second floor of a nondescript building, with red wallpaper
and embarrassing frilly curtains. I remember the windows
had metal bars, to prevent inebriated customers from falling
onto the street. There was a piano, and a young man playing,
which made me wince in a gentle way, as he could so easily
have been me a few years back. Kip's friends were a bit
boring, and we both knew we weren't going to stay terribly
long, just enough to be polite. Kip had developed a terrible
headache, and I offered to go out to a nearby Walgreens and
buy him some aspirin, and then we could say our goodbyes.
So I left the Upstairs Lounge on Chartres Street in The
Quarter in New Orleans on a blistering hot summer night,
and never returned to the world as it had been.

Walgreens was crowded; it took about twenty minutes to
purchase the aspirin. When I returned to Chartres Street,
there was an awful odor. And then I saw the cause; smoke
was billowing out of the building that housed The Upstairs
Lounge. During my absence, the place had been torched.
Literally. Someone had spread petrol on the wooden steps
and set it ablaze. The club was an inferno within seconds.
Firemen were already at the scene; they stopped me from
running into the burning building, I kept yelling Kip's name,
as if the sound of my voice would keep his flesh from melting,
as though my cries would cause the flames to mysteriously
pack up and go home. Afterward, he was identified by tiny
fragments of hair, hair that I would recognize anywhere, hair
that I loved to touch, hair that *he* loved to touch, hair that
would soon be starting a long journey to middle age and
oblivion, but not now, not ever. He was one of the lucky ones;
one man's charred corpse could be seen for the next day
wedged in a window, clutching desperately onto the iron bars.
Thirty-two people died that night, that hot Sunday night way
down yonder . . . Well. Not much more to say. The police
made little effort to find the perpetrator; it was after all, in the
words of a police official, "a queer bar". The newspapers
treated the event as a bit of a party; they said the bodies were
"stacked up like pancakes" and a local disc jockey wondered
if the victims' remains were to be contained in "fruit jars."
Every church of every denomination refused to hold services
for the dead. Not a single local or state official issued a
statement of sympathy. And four families refused to accept
the remains of their loved ones. I didn't collect Kip's remains,
I had not planned on his being cremated quite like this. So. A
bit of history I thought I would "share" with you. Anyhow,
that was then, that was forty years ago. That was Kip. And
that was the explanation for my own charred remains. I left
New Orleans the next day; that time, forever.

The rest is mundane. I was beyond help for a few years. I
drowned in my own misery. You can imagine the details.
Then one night, back in New York, I ran into Jimmy

Baldwin. He registered the state I was in, and he had heard
about Kip. He said, "Baby, what the fuck are you doing
to yourself?" And then he told me about one of Mabel's
recordings, one that I played piano on. He said he had studied
the recording; I didn't believe him, but he went on to analyze
every note and chord I had played, he actually heard what no
one hears when they hear a singer—the accompaniment—
heard and remembered and appreciated. He said "OK, baby,
you're not a genius, you ain't Miles, but you have a talent,
and that's nothing to sneeze at. Shouldn't you show it some
respect?"

He suggested I go to Paris, he gave me the names of a few
clubs there, and so I got myself together, it was really the only
sensible thing to do, and I got on with it, it being life, but
I knew the rules now, I knew the lessons, I knew what not to
expect. So I survived decently in Paris and then I met George
and of course it all happened again and I was reminded of
what life, for a queer boy, was meant to be. That was part of
your attraction, Rufus. I never had to worry about whether it
would end. I knew. It was always impossible. It was as it was.

So here I am, a best man, giving a speech. Which is meant to
be about the two of you. Some chance! I know you're meant
to cry at weddings, and I did, but what exactly was I crying
for, *who* was I crying for? Were my tears for a long-haired
beauty who worshipped a pansy entertainer of decades
before? Were they for a lopsided visionary who took
unsatisfactory Sophocles to Greek islands? Were they for all
the odd creatures who, even if they dressed in suits and had
respectable middle-class jobs, were somehow apart from the
center and were in various ways made to pay for it? Or was I
crying because that was now possibly over, because we were
no longer odd, no longer outlaws, and were now like
everyone else? But why would that be something to shed tears
over? And I can't say that I really know why I've told you
about Kip. I don't know why I think you should carry that
kind of history with you. Baggage can be very heavy—and
destructive—especially if you obsessively cling to it. Well,

maybe clinging is not a great idea. Maybe you should let go.
Or at least accept. *And go on.* OK—here is a reason for going
on. Seeing you happy. Both of you. Well, you've always
argued you had a right to be so. I took that for naivety, for
youth. But now I'm forced to consider that you were merely
asserting a basic desire that people without excess scar tissue
are able to see they deserve. And now I must also consider
that here is something that might work, something that might
last, something that might not be destroyed; at least not
destroyed by history; the vagaries of human interaction will
do whatever they have to do, but that's different. I never
imagined I'd be in a position to say this, but my beloved,
inquisitive, hyperactive Rufus, and dear, sweet, tattooed
Harry, go in some kind of peace, I give you my benediction,
and Kip does as well, and George, and all the shadows, all the
ghosts of peculiar men and singular women, we bless you,
and you must carry our blessings, for whatever they are
worth, carry them with you, and yes, from time to time,
remember where they came from. That's all. I think maybe
you have a chance.

*Lights up on front room. 2014.*

**Harry** *is sitting, next to a pram. He holds a five-month-old baby girl
in his arms.*

**Harry**   What do you want now? A smile? Here's a smile.
Look, Evelyn, Daddy is smiling. You too? You too, honey . . .

*He rubs his face against hers. She makes a sound.*

What was that? Were you crying or laughing? I used to
wonder that about my audiences. Evelyn, Evelyn, Evelyn . . .

**Beau** *and* **Rufus** *come in from the bedroom.*

**Harry**   Did you fix it?

**Rufus**   I can't quite figure it out. The printer just doesn't
start. He needs to print his boarding pass.

**Beau**   I need to print my boarding pass.

**Harry**    I guess you need to print your boarding pass. Doesn't he, Evelyn? Uncle Beau's boarding pass?

**Beau** (*makes a face*)    Eww . . . Uncle Beau.

**Harry**    Would you prefer Gramps?

**Beau**    Thanks.

**Rufus**    Actually, it should be Uncle Beauregard. That scans perfectly. I knew sooner or later your full name would fit something.

**Harry**    Do you like that, Evelyn? Uncle Beauregard?

**Evelyn** *makes a sound.*

**Harry**    She loves it.

**Rufus** *bends down next to* **Evelyn** *and* **Harry**, *and tickles her cheek.*

**Harry** (*to* **Beau**)    Thanks for turning off the heat.

**Beau**    It's July.

**Harry**    That never mattered before.

**Rufus** (*holding* **Evelyn** *and swinging her gently*)    So, Uncle Beauregard, hasn't she grown?

**Beau**    She's virtually Dolly Parton.

**Rufus**    I want to have another go at that boarding pass. I wish you weren't making this trip by yourself.

**Beau**    I'm a big boy. Anyhow, it's your fault. You found out about the anniversary.

**Harry** (*takes* **Evelyn** *from* **Rufus**)    He's going to a jazz funeral, Evelyn, a jazz funeral. Do you know what that is? (*Mimes jazz instruments.*)

**Beau**    Forty some years too late.

**Rufus**    Well, it's about time they commemorated what happened. At least it's something.

**Beau**    I suppose.

**Rufus**    You're certain you won't let me tell them . . .

**Beau**    No, I just want to be there. Quietly. I don't want to be interviewed. I don't want to have to talk. I can't think of anything worse than people coming up to me and saying, "Oh wow, you're a survivor of the Upstairs Lounge." It's nobody's business. I wish to be unobserved. How do I know what I'm going to feel?

**Rufus**    You want . . .

**Beau**    Don't say that word!

**Rufus**    Closure!

**Beau**    That does it. That spoils everything. I'm not going.

**Harry** (*to* **Evelyn**)    Uncle Beauregard's a diva, honey. (*To* **Rufus**.) We really have to make the music decision.

**Rufus** (*to* **Beau**)    What music should she be listening to?

**Harry**    It will affect her for life. I had been thinking classical, for a bit, then something with a real beat, because babies should dance, you know, but actually, I hadn't thought about jazz, there's purity in that . . .

**Rufus**    Maybe Mabel.

**Beau**    Just what she needs. Hidden meanings at five months.

**Harry**    Uncle Beauregard's going to make a list of suggestions for us, honey.

**Beau**    I am?

**Harry**    You are. (*To* **Rufus**.) Where's the sterilizer?

**Rufus**    It was in the car.

**Harry**    You didn't bring it?

**Rufus**    No, you said you would.

**Harry**    I never said that.

**Rufus**    Harry!

**Harry**    You can't just amble away from the car without checking that you have everything.

**Rufus**    As you parked the car without us, I would have assumed you'd be the one to do the final check. Where's the car?

**Harry**    About six and a half minutes away.

**Rufus** (*to* **Evelyn**)    Daddy's going to the car. He'll be back in thirteen minutes.

**Harry**    Will you be all right with her?

**Rufus**    Yes, dear. I can handle it.

**Harry**    Just asking.

**Rufus**    Well, don't.

**Harry**    Right. I'll get it. Have you forgotten anything else?

*Checks through the stuff surrounding the pram.*

**Rufus**    Have *you*?

**Harry** (*to* **Evelyn**)    Don't worry, Daddy's only gone a short time. Come on, honey, smile back at Daddy. That's right.

**Evelyn** *makes a sound.* **Harry** *smiles. He leaves.* **Rufus** *takes* **Evelyn** *in his arms.*

**Rufus**    No one told me it's really hard to be normal.

**Beau**    You should have asked.

**Rufus**    He dotes on her.

**Beau**    Clearly. I'd say he's *addicted* to her.

**Rufus**    Don't.

**Beau**    Sorry. How are you getting along with the notes?

**Rufus** (*cradling* **Evelyn**)    Fine. Well, mostly. Sometimes I have problems with the handwriting. Do you think you could bear to go through some of it with me?

**Beau**    No.

**Rufus**    OK. I'll get there. Kip's penmanship isn't that bad. Do you think I'm crazy doing this?

**Beau**    Not if it allows your obsession with the past to have some . . .

**Rufus**    Relevance, don't say it. I never, ever wanted to be *relevant*. Anyhow, I don't have that much time, between Evelyn and work. The funny thing is my writing Kip's book about Jean Malin was Harry's idea, but now he's the one who's threatened by it. Anything that takes time away from Evelyn . . .

**Beau**    He'll calm down.

**Rufus**    I don't know. He's taking a leave from performing. Just wants to stay home for her first few years. Years!! If there's one virtue to my friggin' law office, it means I can afford a nanny, you know what I mean? He won't hear of it.

*Pause.*

Do you think we should have done this?

**Beau**    My darling, nothing in my life has prepared me for that kind of question.

**Rufus**    I know, I know. Sorry.

*Pause.*

I've got to get your printer going. Take Evelyn.

**Beau**    *What?!*

**Rufus**    Take Evelyn. Hold Evelyn.

**Beau**    *Hold* . . .

**Rufus**    Oh come on, haven't you ever held a baby?

**Beau**    No, actually.

**Rufus**    Well, if you're gonna be Uncle Beauregard, you'll have to. I'm counting on you as babysitter.

**Beau**    Ah. I see.

**Rufus**    Well, we're going to have to *go out*, I mean, every so often; Harry doesn't quite realize what it will do to us if we don't, and you're just about the only person he trusts, so you better start learning how to hold a child . . .

*He hands* **Evelyn** *to* **Beau.**

**Rufus** (*to* **Evelyn**)    It's all right, honey, Papa's going into the next room, but here's Uncle Beauregard. You can drool on Uncle Beauregard. He loves Evelyn's drool, I promise you he does. (*To* **Beau.**) See, it's easy. Doesn't it feel good?

**Beau**    I don't know yet. I'm afraid . . .

**Rufus**    Of what?

**Beau**    Of dropping her.

**Rufus**    I know, the first few weeks I was petrified of doing something wrong, the slightest misstep could be disastrous. And then I realized I wasn't ever going to drop her. I wasn't because I *mustn't*. I think that's the first big lesson I've learned about being a parent. OK. Just shout if you need anything.

*Looks at* **Beau** *holding* **Evelyn.**

**Rufus**    You know, the awful thing is, within a few years, she'll prefer you to Harry and me.

*He goes into the other room.* **Beau** *sits in a chair, and cradles the baby.*

**Beau**    Well, well, well, Evelyn . . .

*Pause.*

Tell me, should we stay in the European Union?

**Evelyn** *makes a sound.*

**Beau** (*shouts, to* **Rufus**)    She's making noises.

**Rufus** (*from the other room*)    Make noises back.

**Beau**    I can't do that.

*Pause.*

Oh Evelyn! When does talking begin? I declare—you *are* drooling. In some quarters, that would be viewed as flirtation.

*Tickles her nose.*

I concede. You're adorable. (*Shouts.*) What do I do now?

**Rufus** (*from the other room*)    Sing to her.

**Beau**    I was afraid of that. When you're a bit older, Evelyn, I'll play the piano for you, just for you, secret songs . . .

**Evelyn** *makes a noise.*

**Beau**    Is that crying? Shh, darling, shh!

*Pause.*

OK . . . Let's rock a bit . . .

*Rocks her slowly and sings.*

Row, row, row your boat . . .

*Pause.*

Who ever would'a thought?

*Sings again.*

Row, row, row your boat
Gently down the stream
Merrily, merrily, merrily, merrily . . .

*A long pause.*

Life is but a dream.

*Curtain.*

For a complete listing of Bloomsbury
Methuen Drama titles, visit:

**www.bloomsbury.com/drama**

Follow us on Twitter and keep up to date
with our news and publications

**@MethuenDrama**